ABC

FOLDER GAMES

PATTERNS FOR EASY-TO-DO
READING GAMES

by Lillian Lieberman, illustrated by Marilynn G. Barr

Publisher: Roberta Suid
Editor: Carol Whiteley
Production: Susan Cronin-Paris

Entire contents copyright ©1991 by Monday Morning
Books, Inc., Box 1680, Palo Alto, California 94302

Monday Morning is a registered trademark of
Monday Morning Books, Inc.

ISBN 1-878279-29-7

Printed in the United States of America
9 8 7 6 5 4 3 2

For a complete catalog, write to the address above.

Contents

Introduction

ABC Folder Games provides easy-to-use, enjoyable readiness and pre-academic skills activities for children ages pre-school to kindergarten. The book utilizes file folder set-ups and is designed for instruction by teachers and parents.

The activities in ABC Folder Games motivate and reinforce beginning reading skills in an easy and useable format. The children discriminate among cutout shapes, develop letter skills by matching upper- and lower-case letters, and will enjoy matching letters on poker chips to pictures on gumballs that begin with the same consonant sound. They'll also make a giant pizza by sorting out rhyming words with picture clues, and use yarn lengths to match pictures that are in the same category.

Each file folder activity includes the necessary layout and the activity sheets to be duplicated. A list of readily available materials, easy construction steps, and directions for the activities are also given. A number of simple worksheets that reinforce the skills covered are provided.

The varied activities in ABC Folder Games will suit a wide range of student needs and abilities. The children will enjoy using the folders individually or in small groups, and the activities can also be part of learning stations or centers. As an added learning incentive, the book supplies bulletin board ideas and enrichment activities for individual or group involvement.

General Directions

Construction

Colored file folders are suggested for making these activities, but any sturdy file folders will do. Washable felt markers are recommended for coloring and marking on laminated surfaces to avoid bleeding into the activity sheets.

Trim all the activity sheets slightly smaller than the file folder before you glue them to the folder and seal them with plastic laminate sheeting. Use a laminating kit available from educational supply companies or have the laminating done professionally at a picture frame shop. Or you may purchase sheets of laminate from office supply stores or use clear Contact paper. As an alternative to laminating you can use clear plastic sleeves into which you slip the activity sheets.

After construction, be sure to mark each manila envelope glued to a file folder with its contents in case some of the parts are misplaced.

Activities

File folder activities are ideal for use at learning centers or work stations. They are designed as supplementary and enrichment experiences to give your children added skills reinforcement. Encourage the children to use the activities after their classroom work is finished, or at particular, set times. They will be able to do the activities with only a little guidance. After a child works on a laminated surface, have him or her wipe the surface clean for the next person using a tissue, dampened slightly if necessary.

Look Out for b and d!

Children track for b and d in left to right orientation and name and trace b and d patterns.

Objective: To reinforce directional orientation and to discriminate between b and d

Materials: File folder, title sheet, activity sheets, 9" x 6" manila envelope with fastener, water-base felt pens, poster board, rubber cement, plastic laminate, clear plastic sealing tape, craft knife or scissors

Preparation: Duplicate the title and activity sheets. Use the felt pens to color the title sheet and the balls, fish, and duck on the activity sheets. Color the clear circles red on the large letter patterns b and d. Glue the large letter patterns to poster board and laminate. Cut into two parts on the dotted line. Glue the title sheet to the folder front and glue the two sheets of tracing activities to the inside of the folder. Laminate the folder inside and outside. Glue the manila envelope to the folder back and secure with the sealing tape. Store the large letter patterns in the envelope.

Activity: Show the class the folder title illustration to illustrate the way many children remember how the b and d are positioned. Let the children duplicate the bed illustration with their clenched fists touching, thumbs pointing up. Also have them practice writing the letters in the air, naming them each time. Then have the children trace the small d's and b's on the activity sheets with water-base felt pens, tracking each letter starting at the ball. Have them start each letter row at the left and work toward the right. Have them trace the large letter patterns starting at the red dot and follow the arrows for more motor-sequencing practice. Ask the children to name the letter each time they trace one.

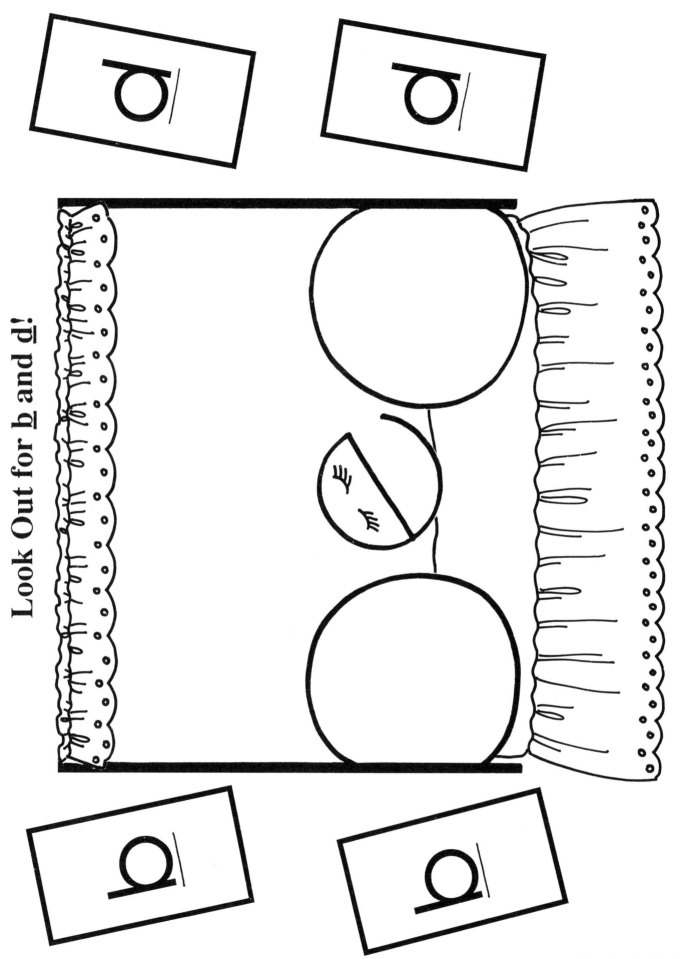

Look Out for <u>b</u> and <u>d</u>!

Trace all the d's to the duck. Start at the little ball each time.

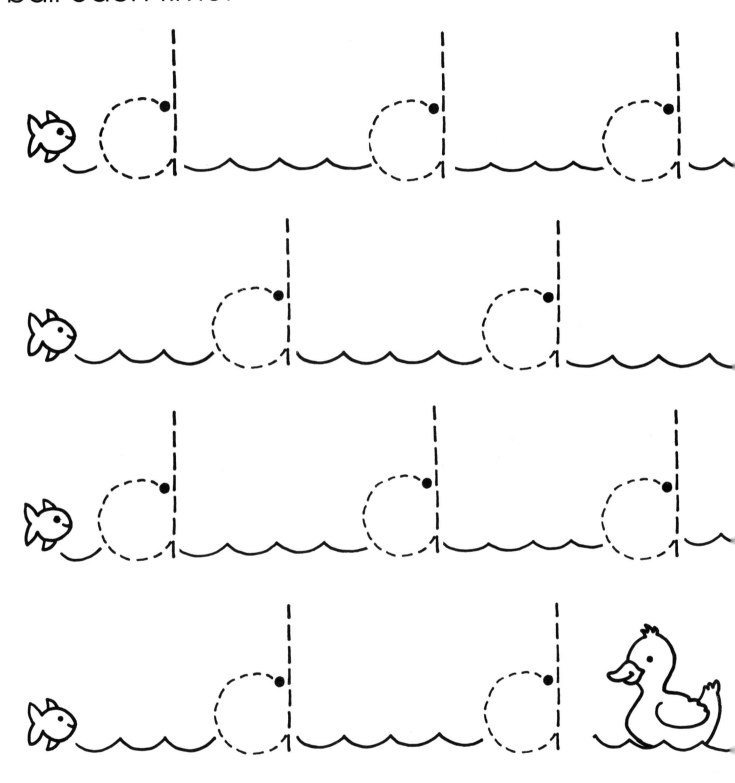

Trace all the b's to the big ball. Start at the little ball each time.

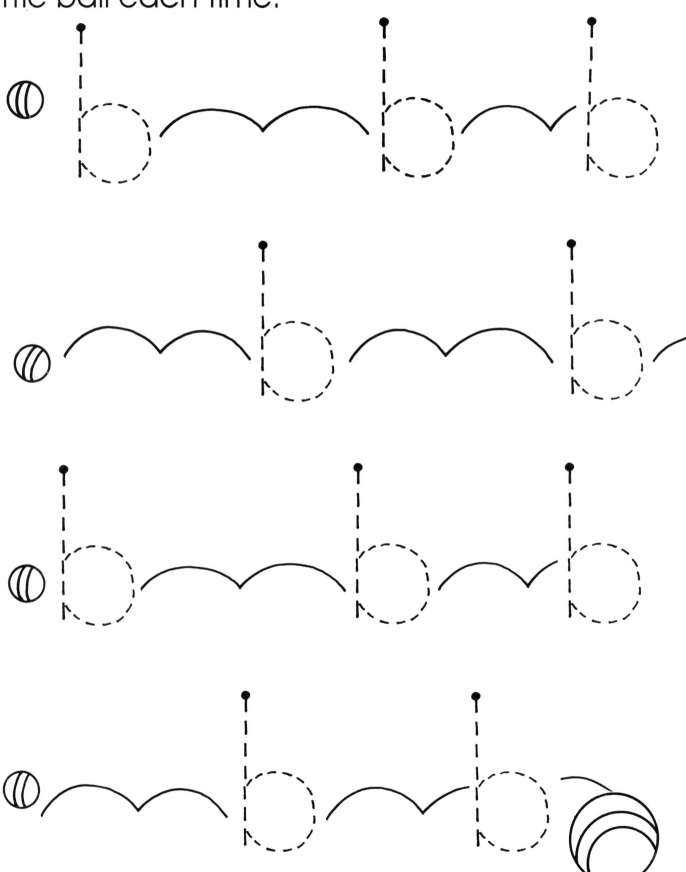

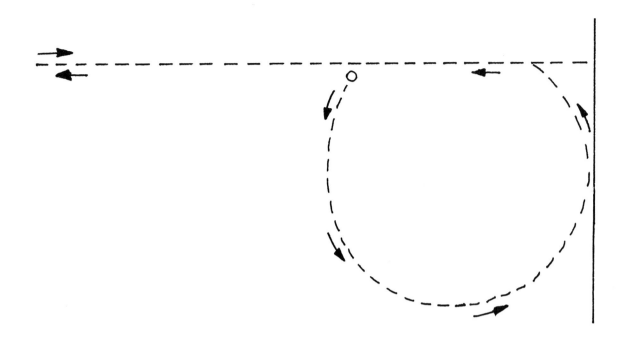

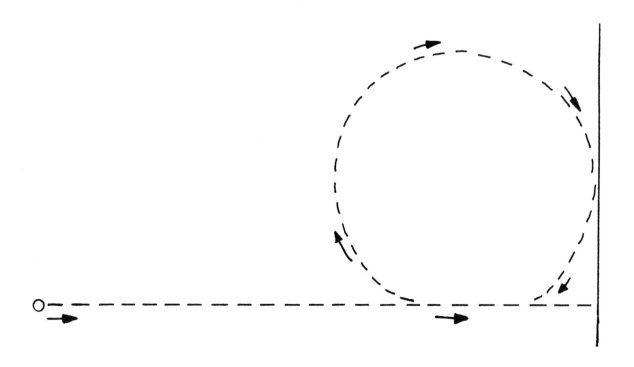

Grandma's Cookies

Children match upper- and lower-case letters of the alphabet and get extra turns to play if they choose Grandma's cookies.

Objective: To reinforce upper- and lower-case letter association

Materials: File folder, title sheet, activity sheets, 9" x 6" manila envelope with fastener, water-base felt pens, poster board, rubber cement, plastic laminate, clear plastic sealing tape, craft knife or scissors

Preparation: Duplicate the title sheet and the activity sheets. Color the title sheet and the cookies on the activity sheets. Glue the title sheet to the folder front and glue the two sheets of matching activities inside the folder. Glue the upper- and lower-case letter sheets to poster board. Laminate the folder inside and outside and laminate the letter sheets. Cut the letters and cookies apart. Glue the manila envelope to the back of the folder and secure with sealing tape. Store the letter and cookie cards inside and fasten.

Activity: Have the children use the water-base felt pens to draw lines that match upper- and lower-case letters on the activity sheets. To play a game with the cards, separate the lower-case from the upper-case cards. Include the cookie cards with the lower-case letters. Place the lower-case cards face down in one pile and the upper-case cards face down in rows. Have each of two children take four cards from the pile and place them face up. Then have them take a card, one child at a time, from the face-down rows. If the card matches one of their lower-case cards, they place it on top. If there is no match, the card is returned to the row. If a cookie card is picked, the child gets an extra turn. The one who makes all his or her matches first wins.

© 1991 Monday Morning Books, Inc.

Match the letters. Draw a line.

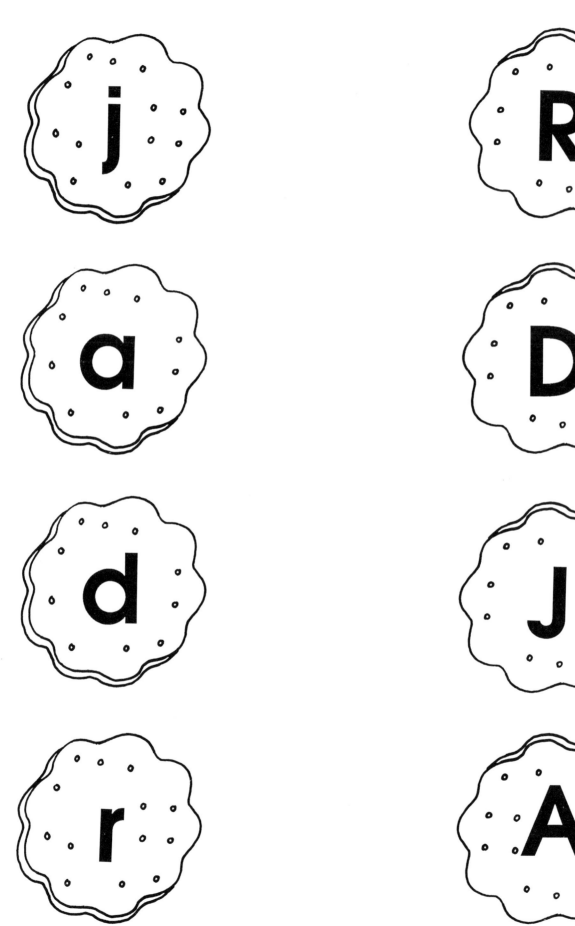

Match the letters. Draw a line.

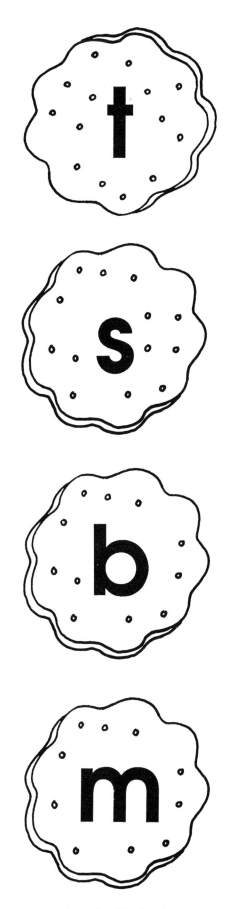
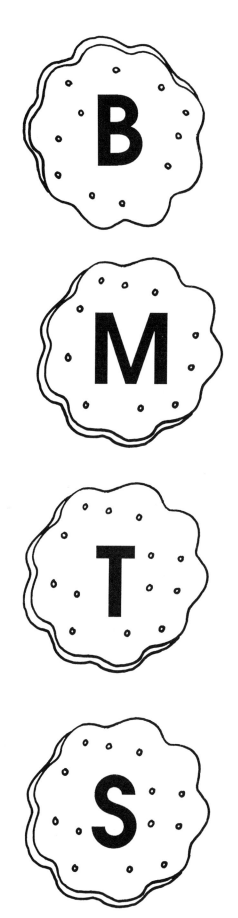

13

e	j	o
d	i	n
c	h	m
b	g	l
a	f	k

t	s	r	q	p
Y	X	W	V	U
D	C	B	A	Z

I	N	S
H	M	R
G	L	Q
F	K	P
E	J	O

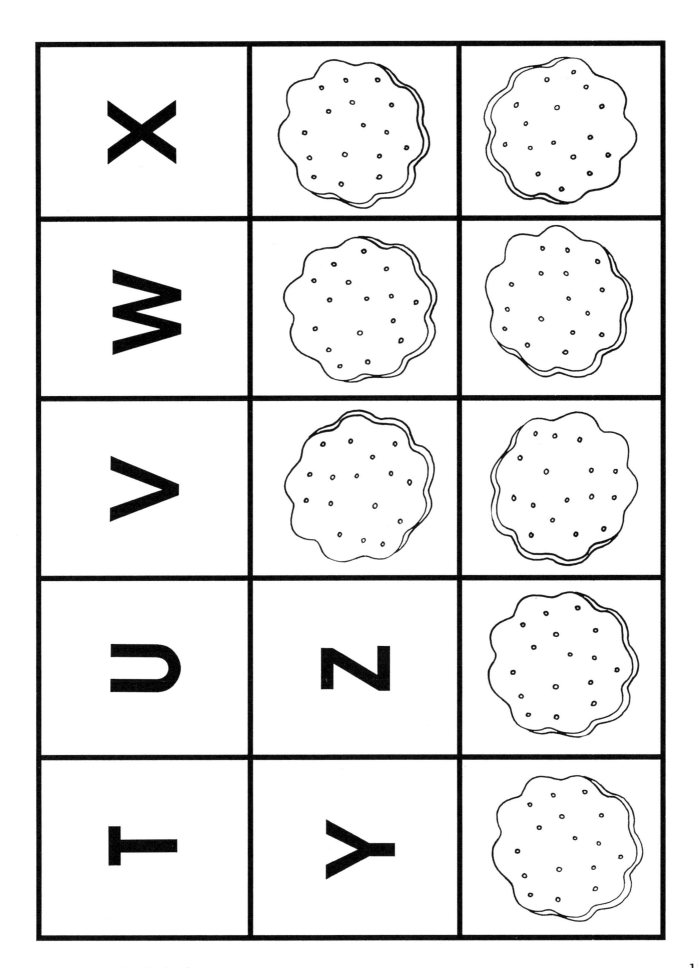

The Big Cheese

Children help the mouse reach the big piece of cheese and get safely back to the mouse hole by tracking the alphabet in order.

Objective: To reinforce alphabetical sequence

Materials: File folder, title sheet, activity sheets, 9" x 6" manila envelope with fastener, water-base felt pens, poster board, rubber cement, plastic laminate, clear plastic sealing tape, craft knife or scissors

Preparation: Duplicate the title sheet and the activity sheets. Color the title sheet and the activity sheets with directions with felt pens. Glue the title sheet to the folder front. Glue the activity sheets with directions inside the folder and the sheet without directions to poster board. Laminate the folder inside and outside and laminate the sheet glued to poster board. Cut the sheet on the poster board on the dotted line to form two game cards. Glue the manila envelope to the back of the folder and secure with tape. Store the game cards in the envelope.

Activity: To work on the activity sheets, have the children use the water-base pens to connect the mouse's prints in alphabetical order. Have them name the letters as they track both the upper- and lower-case sequences. To play with the game cards, have the children connect the dots in alphabetical order to complete the drawing of the cheese. Have them name the letters as they track the upper- and lower-case sequences.

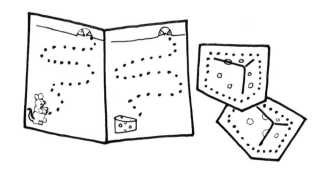

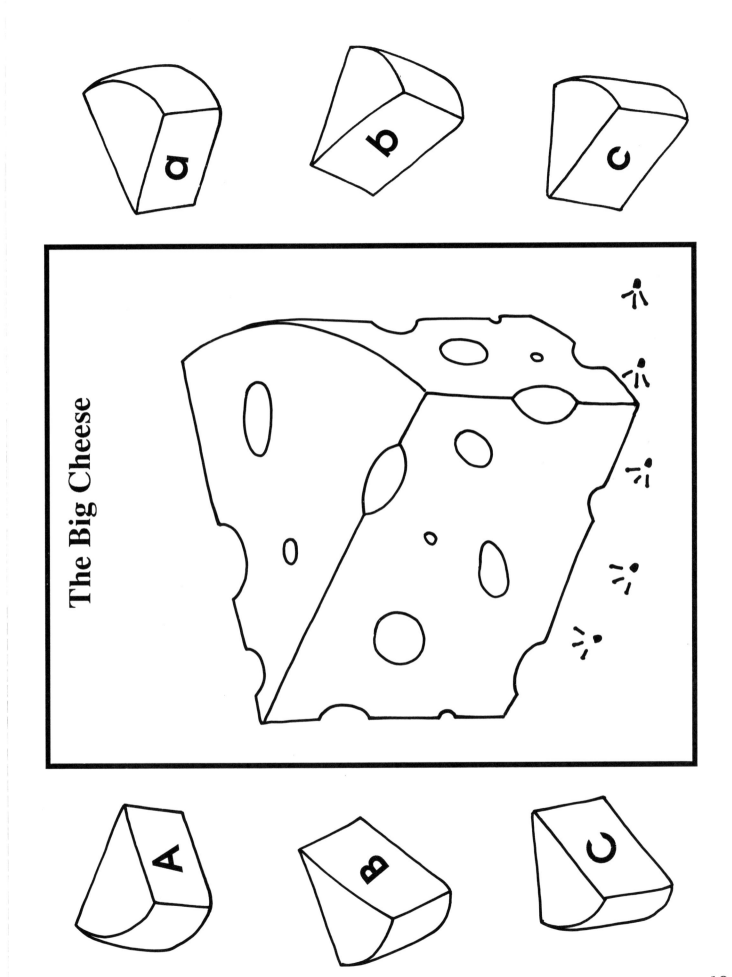

The Big Cheese

19

Trace the abc way to the cheese.
Name each letter as you go.

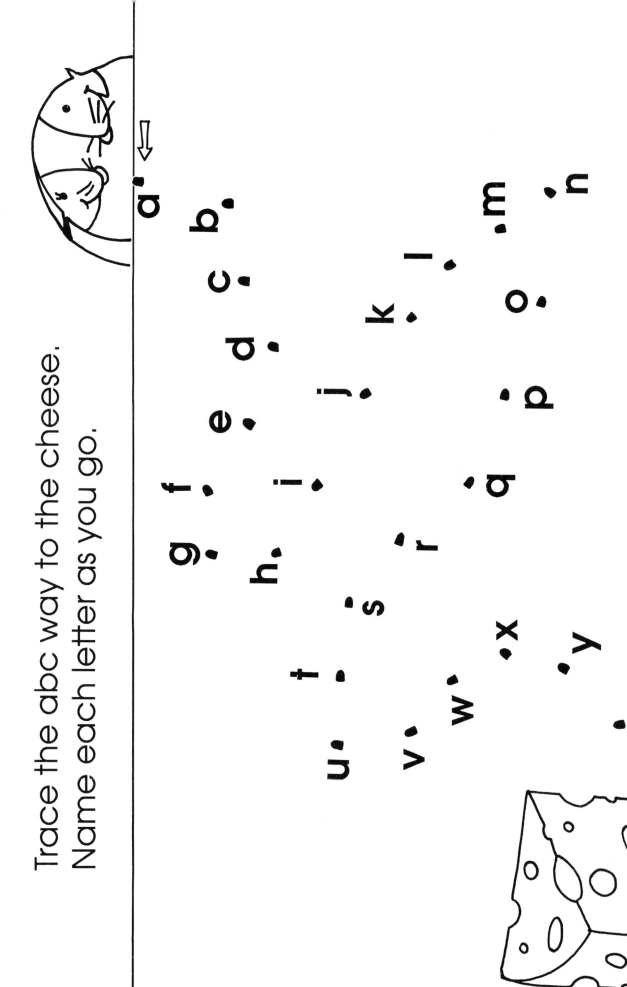

20

Trace the ABC way to the mouse hole.
Name each letter as you go.

N· O· P· Q· R· S· T· U·
M· L· K· J· I· H· G·
B· C· D· E· F·
→·A·
X· Y· Z·
W· V·

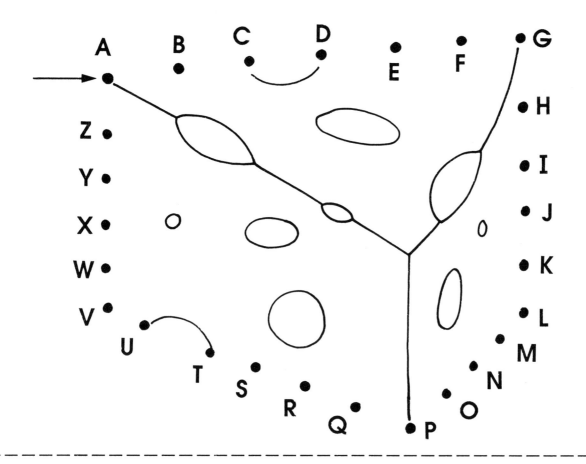

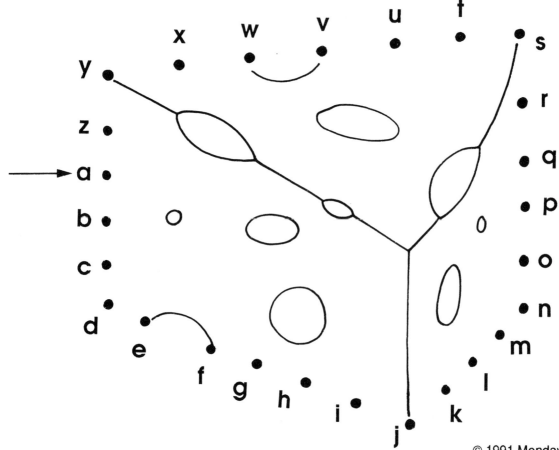

Juggling Clown

Children help the juggling clown fill in missing letters in alphabetical sequences.

Objective: To reinforce alphabetical sequence

Materials: File folder, title sheet, activity sheets, 9" x 6" manila envelope with fastener, water-base felt pens, poster board, rubber cement, plastic laminate, clear plastic sealing tape, craft knife or scissors

Preparation: Duplicate the title sheet and the activity sheets, making two copies of the activity sheet without directions. Color the title sheet and the clown on the activity sheets with water-base felt pens. Glue the title sheet to the folder front and the two activity sheets with written directions inside the folder. Laminate the folder inside and outside. Glue each of the sheets without directions on poster board and laminate. Cut them apart to make alphabet strips. Glue the manila envelope to the back of the folder and secure with sealing tape. Store the alphabet strips in the envelope and fasten.

Activity: Have the children use the washable pens to fill in the missing letters on the activity sheets. Let two children at a time use the alphabetical sequence strips. Have them place the strips face down in the playing area. Then have each child in turn take a strip and choose additional strips to try to complete the alphabet. If a duplicate strip is taken, it is replaced face down in the playing area. To check for accuracy, ask the children to name the letters in order and check each other's alphabetical sequencing.

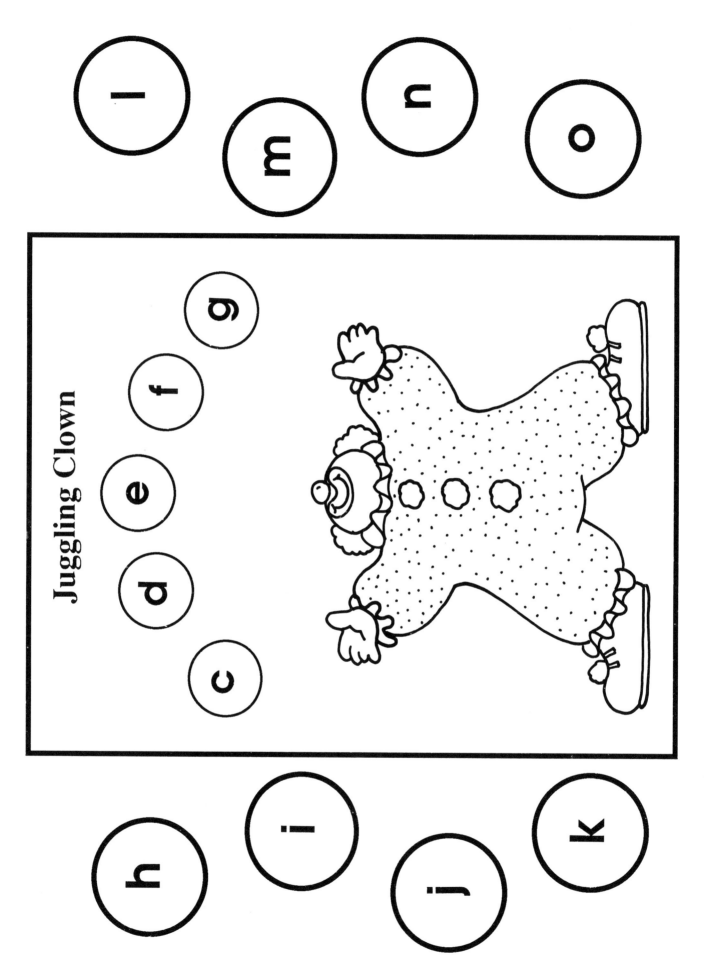

Juggling Clown

Write the missing letter on the ball.

w   r   d   s

Write the missing letter on the ball.

k h m c

g _ i

a b _

_ n o

j _ l

- -

a   b   c   d

- -

e   f   g

- -

h   i   j   k

- -

l   m   n   o   p

- -

q   r   s   t   u

- -

v   w   x   y   z

- -

Gumball Machine

Children identify initial consonant sounds and symbols as they match poker chip letters to pictures on gumballs.

Objective: To reinforce sound-symbol association for initial consonants

Materials: File folder, title sheet, activity sheets, 9" x 6" manila envelope with fastener, water-base felt pens, black permanent marker pen, poster board, 21 poker chips (white or light colored), rubber cement, plastic laminate, clear plastic sealing tape, craft knife or scissors

Preparation: Duplicate the title sheet and the activity sheets. Color them with the water-base pens. Glue the title sheet to the folder front and the two activity sheets with written directions on the inside of the folder. Laminate the folder inside and outside. Use the marker pen to write one consonant on each poker chip; add base lines to prevent confusion.

Glue the remaining activity sheet to poster board and laminate. Cut on the dotted line to make two game cards. Glue the manila envelope to the back of the folder and secure with clear sealing tape. Store the game cards and the poker chips in the envelope.

Activity: Give individual children the activity sheets and set the poker chips in rows face up with the base lines aligned. Then have the children name each gumball picture on each activity sheet. Have them find and place the poker chip with the letter for the initial sound on each gumball picture. Two children can play together with the game cards. The first child to correctly match poker chip letters to all his or her gumball pictures wins.

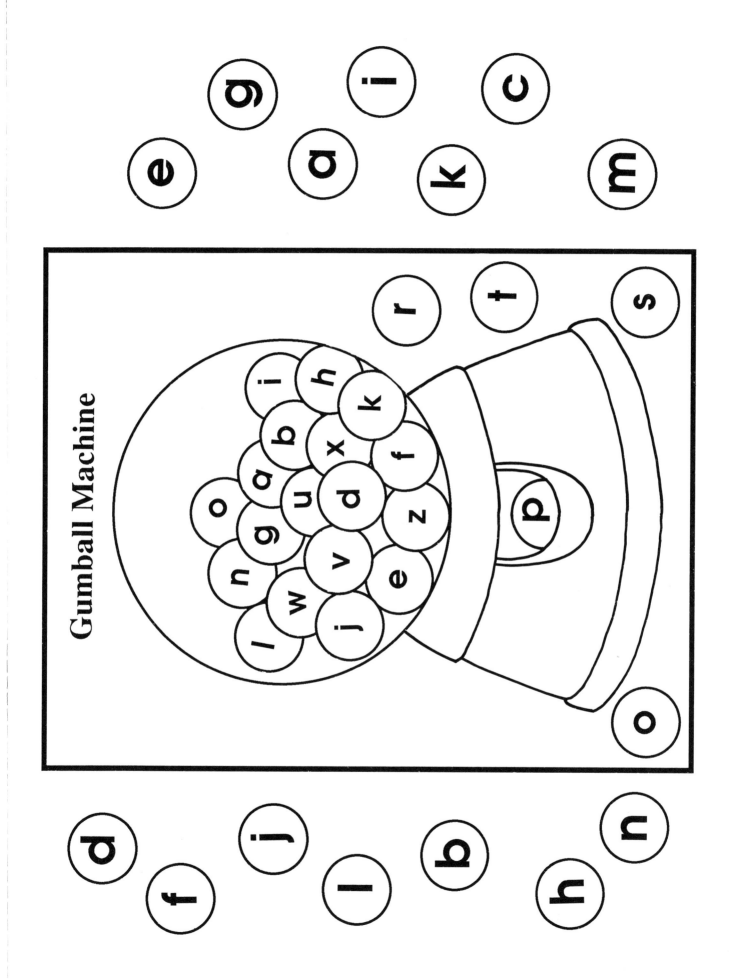

Gumball Machine

Put a letter chip on each picture. Match the chip to the first letter sound of each picture.

Put a letter chip on each picture. Match the chip to the first letter sound of each picture.

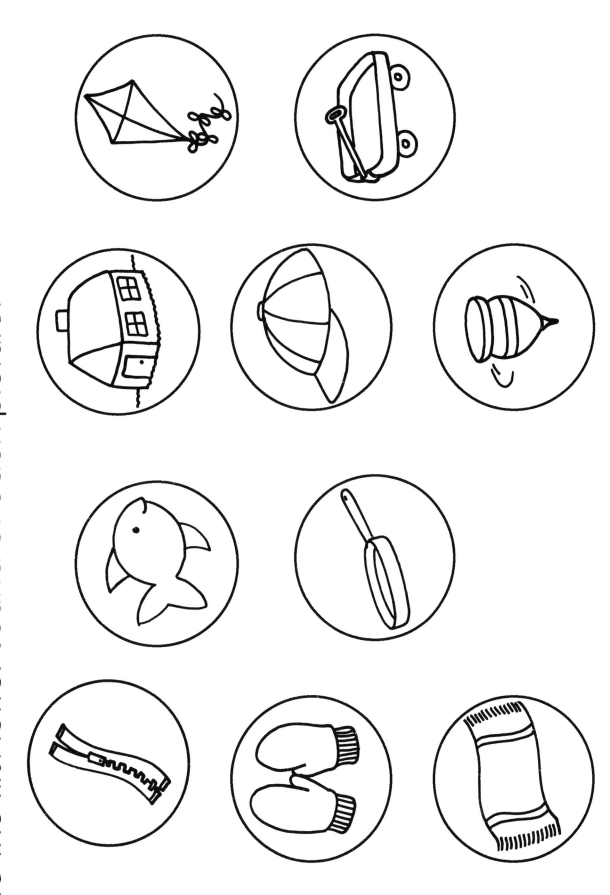

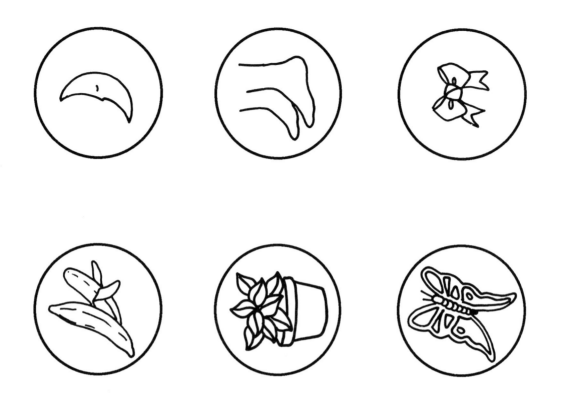

Peas in a Pod

Children identify final consonant sounds and symbols for pictures and write the letters on pea pods. They also match poker chip letters to final sounds for pictures in a game.

Objective: To reinforce sound-symbol association for final consonants

Materials: File folder, title sheet, activity sheets, 9" x 6" manila envelope with fastener, water-base felt pens, black permanent marker pen, poster board, 12 poker chips (white or light colored), rubber cement, plastic laminate, clear plastic sealing tape, craft knife or scissors

Preparation: Duplicate the title sheet and the activity sheets. Color with water-base felt pens. Glue the title sheet to the folder front and the two activity sheets with written directions to the inside of the folder. Laminate the folder inside and outside. Use the permanent marker to write a large consonant letter b, d, f, g, k, l, m, n, p, s, t, or x on each poker chip; add base lines to prevent confusion. Glue the remaining activity sheet to poster board and laminate. Cut in half on the dotted line. Glue the manila envelope to the back of the folder and secure with sealing tape. Store the two game cards and the poker chips in the envelope.

Activity: To use the activity sheets, have the children use the washable pens to write the letter associated with the final sound of each picture on the pea pod. Have them look at the letters at the top of the sheet to guide them if necessary. Let two children play with the two game cards. Set the poker chip letters in a row face up with base lines aligned. Have the children in turn take a poker chip and match the letter to the final sound of one of the pictures on his or her game card.

Peas in a Pod

Write the last letter for each picture.
Use the letters in the box.

d m s x p

Write the last letter for each picture.
Use the letters in the box.

k r n g l

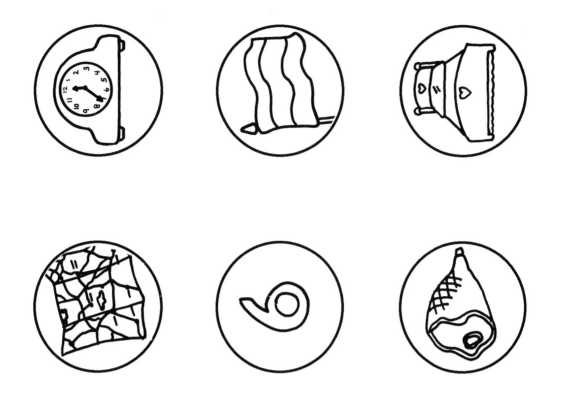

Giant Rhyme Pizza

Children identify and match pictures that rhyme on a giant pizza. On additional activity cards they match pictures on pizza slices to simple words.

Objective: To identify rhyming elements

Materials: File folder, title sheet, activity sheets, 9" x 6" manila envelope, water-base felt pens, poster board, rubber cement, plastic laminate, clear sealing tape, craft knife or scissors

Preparation: Duplicate the title sheet and the activity sheets. Color with water-base felt pens. Glue the title sheet to the folder front. Glue the two sheets of giant pizzas with written directions inside the folder. Laminate the folder inside and outside. Glue the other two sheets of giant pizzas and the sheet of pizza slices to poster board. Laminate. Cut apart the pizza slices on the giant pizzas and cut the sheet of pizza slices on the dotted line to make two activity cards. Glue the manila envelope to the back of the folder and secure with plastic tape. Store the pizza slices and the two activity cards in the envelope.

Activity: Have the children use the washable pens to draw lines on the activity cards from the pictures on the pizzas to the words that have the same rhyme element. To play a game, let the children name and match the pictures on the pizza slices to pictures on the giant pizzas that have the same rhyme element.

rat

jet

hot

Giant Rhyme Pizza

Match the picture on a cut-out pizza slice
with a picture on the pizza that rhymes.
Put the pictures on the pizza.

Match the picture on a cut-out pizza slice with a picture on the pizza that rhymes. Put the pictures on the pizza.

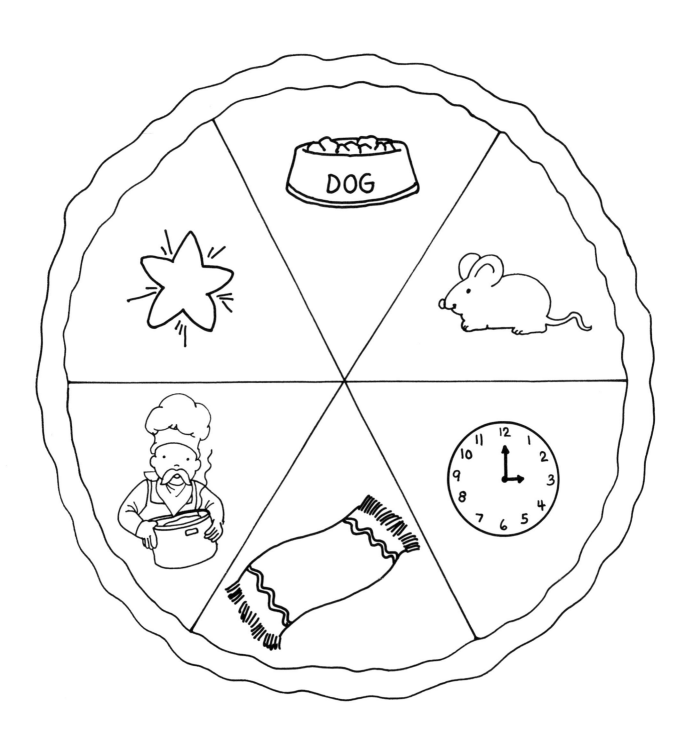

Match the picture to the word
that rhymes. Draw a line.

cut

man

win

Match the picture to the word
that rhymes. Draw a line.

hot

jet

rat

What's the Scoop?

Children match number words to symbols and place the matching number of ice cream scoops on numbered cones.

Objective: To reinforce number sight words

Materials: File folder, title sheet, activity sheets, 9" x 6" manila envelope with fastener, water-base felt pens, poster board, rubber cement, plastic laminate, clear plastic sealing tape, craft knife or scissors

Preparation: Duplicate the title sheet and the activity sheets. Make three copies of the sheet of ice cream scoops. Color the title sheet and the activity sheets with water-base felt pens. Glue the title sheet to the folder front and the sheets with directions inside the folder. Laminate the folder inside and outside. On each sheet of ice cream scoops, draw a star on each of five scoops. Glue all the sheets of scoops and the sheet of cones to poster board and laminate. Cut out the scoops and the cones. Glue the envelope to the back of the folder and store the scoops and cones in it.

Activity: To use the matching activity sheets, have the children draw lines with washable felt pens between number words and number symbols. To play the scoops and cones game, have two children place the cones and the scoops in separate piles face down in a playing area. Let each child in turn take a cone and read the number word on it. Have him or her then pick up that number of ice cream scoops and pile them on the cone. If the child names the number on the cone incorrectly, the cone must be replaced and the child misses a turn. If a child picks up a scoop with a star, he or she may take another cone to play with. The child with the most scoops at the end of the game wins.

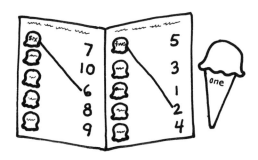

four

five

six

What's the Scoop?

one

one

two

three

Match each scoop to a number. Draw a line between them.

six

nine

seven

ten

eight

7

10

6

8

9

Match each scoop to a number. Draw a line between them.

two   5

four   3

three   1

one   2

five   4

48

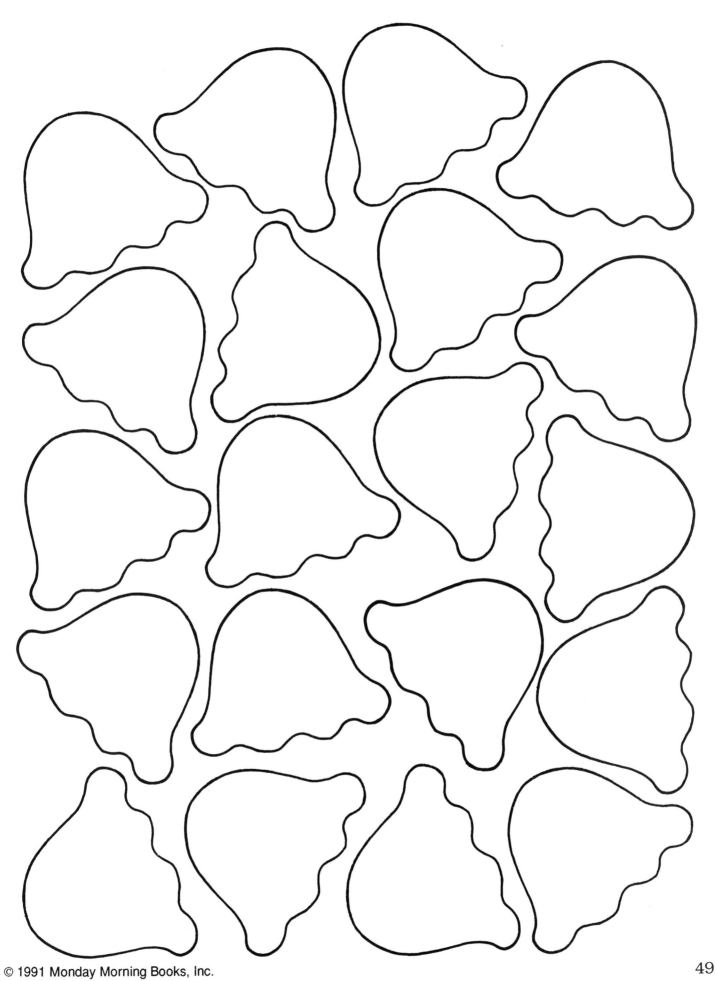

49

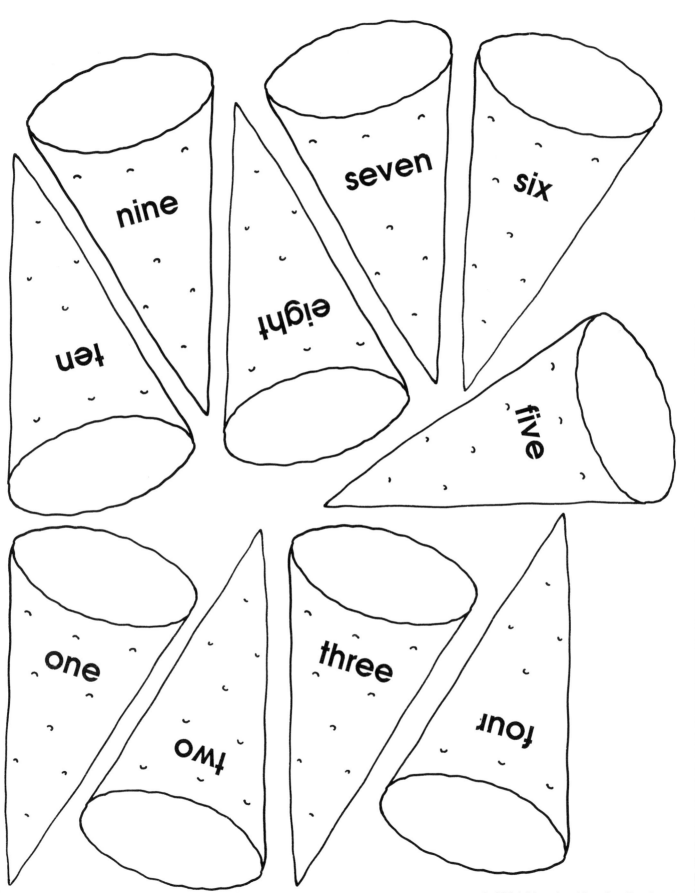

Color Baskets

Children name the colors of objects and match them to color words on baskets.

Objective: To reinforce color sight words

Materials: File folder, title sheet, activity sheets, 9" x 6" manila envelope with fastener, water-base felt pens, poster board, rubber cement, plastic laminate, craft knife or scissors, sealing tape

Preparation: Duplicate the title sheet and the activity sheets, making two copies of the sheet of baskets. Color the title sheet. On the activity sheets with directions, color the food the appropriate colors. On the sheet of picture cards, also color the items the appropriate colors (peppers green, gumballs and Popsicle blue). Glue the title sheet to the folder front. Glue the activity sheets with directions inside the folder. Laminate the folder inside and outside. Laminate the sheet of cards. Cut the cards apart. Glue the two sheets of baskets to poster board. Write either yellow, purple, red, green, brown, blue, white, or orange in the blank on each basket. Laminate the sheets. Cut the baskets apart. Glue the envelope to the back of the folder. Secure with sealing tape. Enclose the baskets and cards.

Activity: On the two activity sheets, let the children draw lines to match color words to colored pictures. To have two children play a game, place the baskets face down in a pile and the picture cards face down in rows. Let each child take a basket. Then, in turn, have the children each take a picture card, name the object's color, and see if it matches the color name on their basket. Matches are placed on the basket. If there's no match, the card is replaced in the row. When a basket is filled with two picture cards, the child may take another basket.

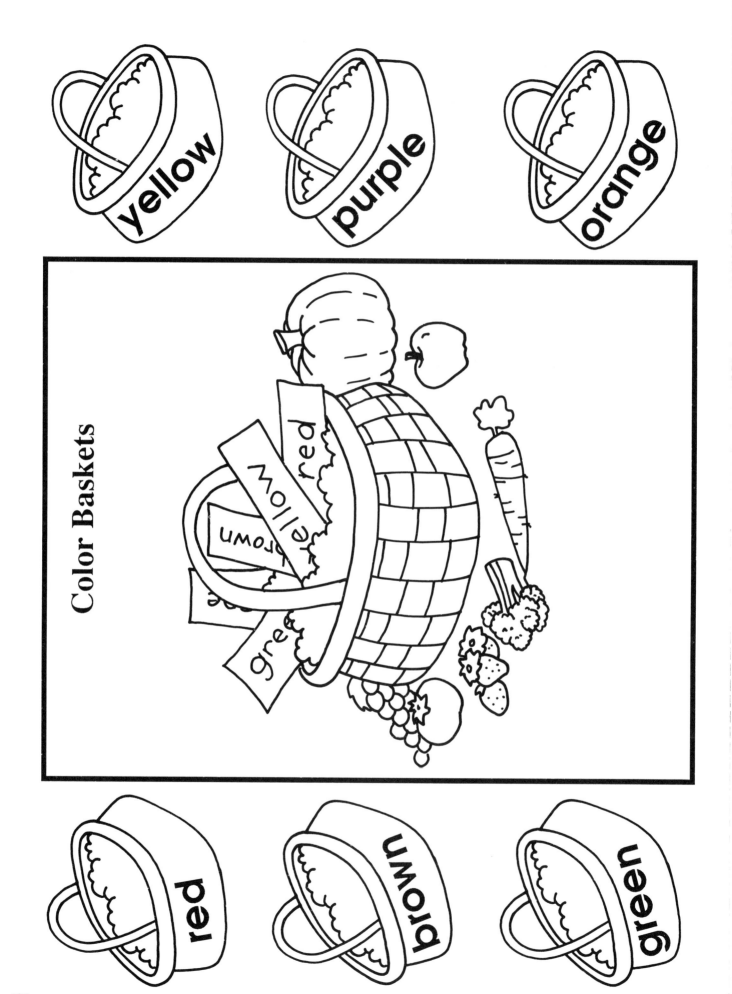

yellow

purple

orange

Color Baskets

red

brown

green

Match each color basket with two pictures. Draw a line between them.

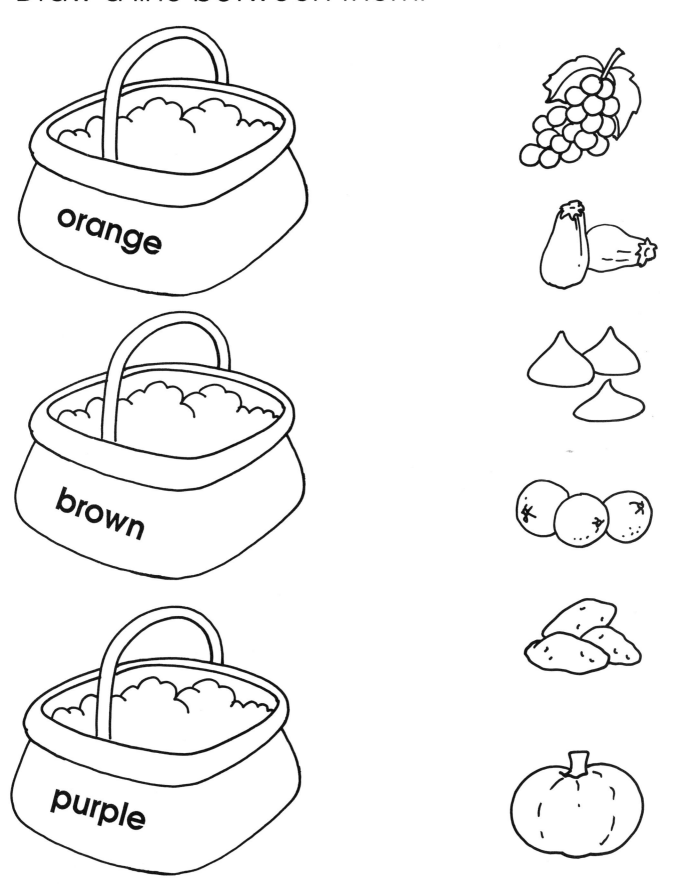

Match each color basket with two pictures. Draw a line between them.

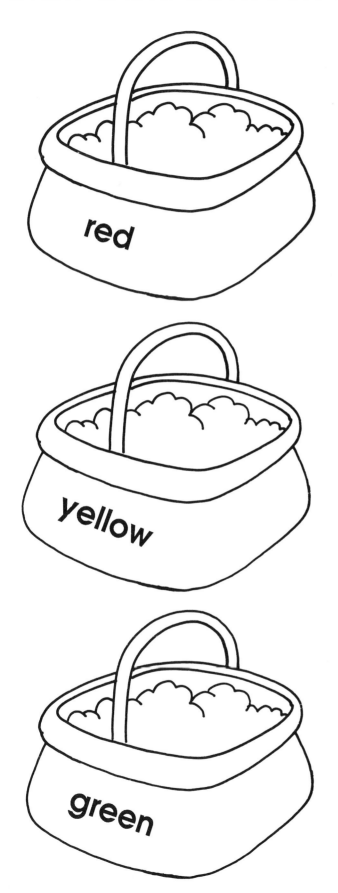

54

Mitten Match

Children match pictures on mittens by common element.

Objective: To reinforce categorizing skills

Materials: File folder, title sheet, activity sheets, 9" x 6" manila envelope with fastener, water-base felt pens, 4 different-colored strands of yarn, poster board, rubber cement, plastic laminate, clear plastic sealing tape, craft knife or scissors, hole punch

Preparation: Duplicate the title sheet and the activity sheets. Color with the pens. Glue the title sheet to the folder front and the activity sheets with directions inside the folder; glue the sheet to be hole punched on the inside back of the folder. Laminate the folder inside and outside. Punch holes on the appropriate activity sheet (use the sharp end of scissors if necessary). Thread a different-colored length of yarn through each hole on the left side, leaving the end free. Color-code the back of the folder with felt pens for self-checking. Glue the mitten sheets to poster board. Laminate and cut apart. Glue the envelope to the back of the folder. Secure with tape. Enclose the mitten cards and fasten.

Activity: To use the activity sheet without yarn, have the children draw a line between mittens with matching elements, for example, between the shirt and the pants because both are clothes. To use the second activity sheet, have children match mittens by threading yarn through the appropriate hole. Have the children name and tell why the pictures on the mittens go together and self-check their answers. Let two children use the mitten cards by placing them face down, then picking up two at a time. If the cards match by category, the child should tell the category and keep the cards. If cards do not match, they must be replaced face down. The child with the most mitten matches wins.

Mitten Match

Match the mittens.
Draw a line between them.

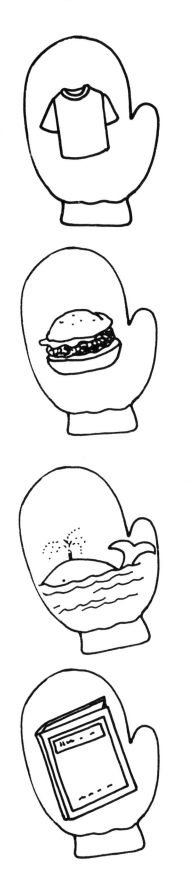

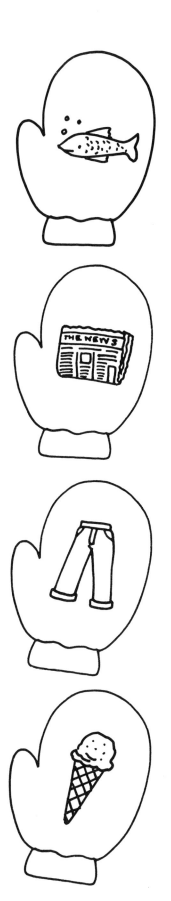

Match the mittens with the yarn.

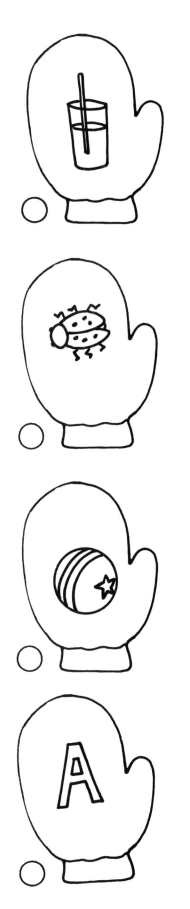

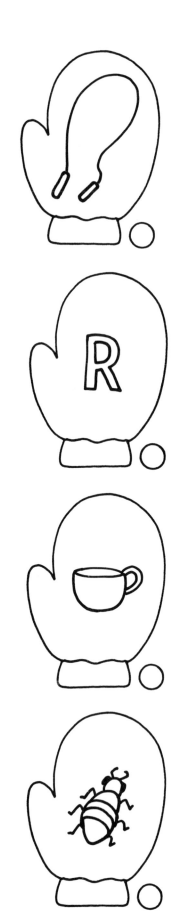

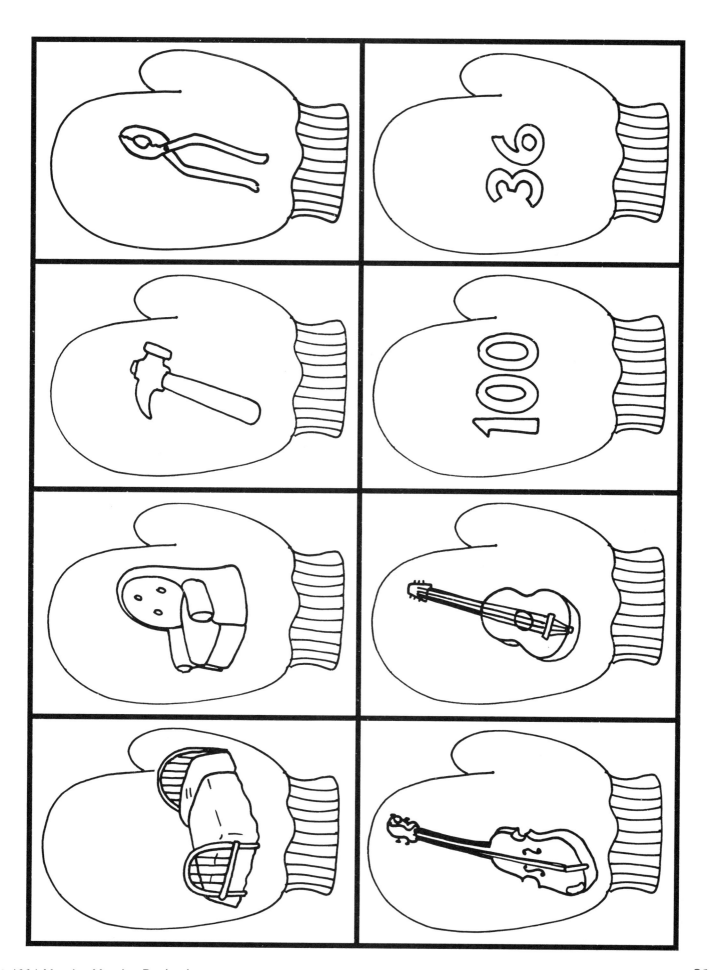

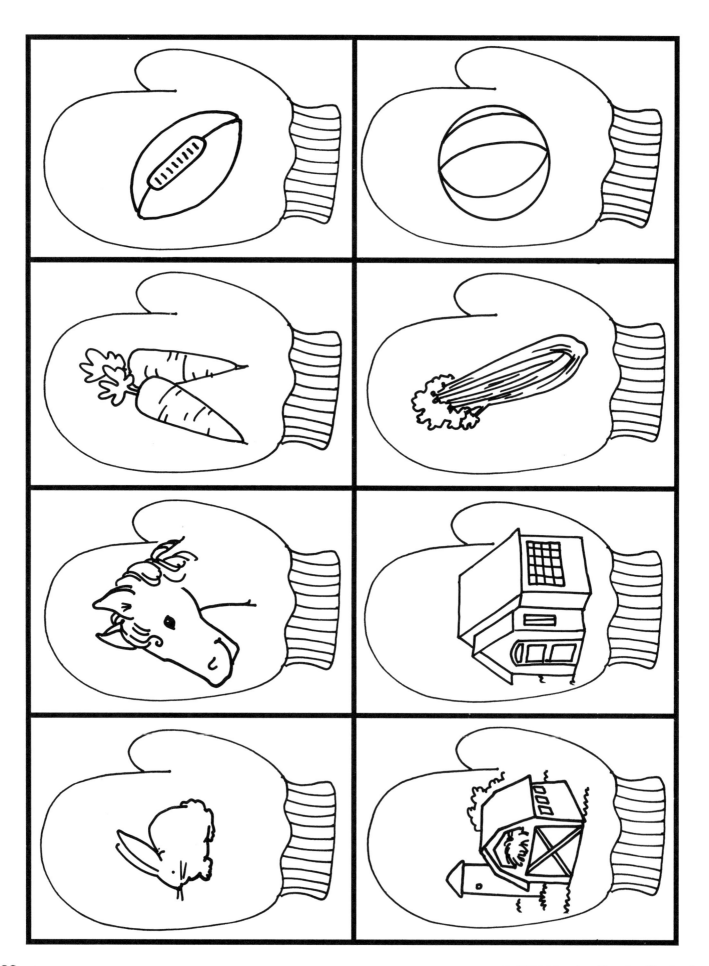

Enrichment Activities

Shapes Feely Box

Tape shut a medium-size box. Cut a round hole in it and tape a cut-off sock to the mouth of the hole. Cover the box with Contact paper. Place various shaped objects in the box and ask the children to reach in through the sock and feel and guess the shape of each object. Let them take the shapes out to check their guesses.

Shape Sorting

Set out a box full of different sizes of several cutout shapes. Make more than one cutout for each shape. Let the children have fun sorting the shapes and using them to create shape designs.

Safari Shape Hunt

Tell the children to pretend they are going on a safari to hunt for shapes. Have them put on imaginary safari hats and walk around the room looking for things with as many different shapes as possible. Have them name each shape they see.

Letter of the Day

Place a blank face with a crown on it on the bulletin board; add a cloth cape if desired for extra effect. Introduce a new letter by placing a cutout of the letter on the blank face, making it king or queen for the day. Plan events around the letter, for example, make jelly sandwiches, play a simple jump rope game, or make J-theme scrapbooks of drawings or pictures for the letter J.

Listen! Guess the Letter!

For beginning sound perception and reinforcement, have a child stand in front of you facing the other children. Say, "Listen! Guess the letter for this sound." Say the sound. Ask the child to guess the letter and, if he or she is correct, give the child a cutout of the letter to keep. If the child guesses incorrectly, say the name of the letter, show the cutout letter, and let the child trace the letter.

What's My Rhyme?

For auditory perception and discrimination for rhyme, tell the children they are to listen for words that rhyme with a particular word you say to them. Read a list of words containing that rhyme element. Ask the children to raise their hands each time they hear a word that rhymes with the target rhyme element.

Upper-case/Lower-case Letter Match

Make sets of upper- and lower-case letters. Have the children sit at their desks with their eyes closed. Tiptoe around and place either an upper-case or a lower-case letter in each child's desk. The children may peek at their letter. Then pick a child to go around the room and ask three classmates if they have the upper- or lower-case match to the child's letter. If the child finds a match, he or she gets another turn. If no match is found, the child with the match gets a turn.

Categorization

Keep a box of objects handy for children to sort by like characteristics, for example, all objects that are round or all objects of the same color. Encourage the children to think of different ways to sort the materials.